# The

# SEX

# ALLEGORY

## (And Other Poems)

## Louisa Lum

Miraclaire Publishing

**MIRACLAIRE PUBLISHING**

P.O. Box 8616, Yaounde 14
Centre Region, Cameroon

*Email:* info@miraclairebooks.com
*Website:* www.miraclairepublishing.com

**Tel:** 237 75 03 72 78

**ISBN-10: 0615487270**

**ISBN-13: 978-0615487274**

**Dedication**

To

Ngumambe Nadia

and

All the Little Angels in the World

With All My Love

# PREFACE

In this debut collection, Louisa Lum shows a mastery of poetic artistry by writing in a variety of styles and subjects. Though not separated, the poems represent two ideological positions.

The first set of poems, written possibly earlier in the poet's career, represents a subject that is more liberal (or do I say universal). They show a penchant to decry the growing misery of the world around the poet and an inclination to criticise the political order for such wretched conditions. The poet is humanist in ideology and at some turn becomes highly philosophical as to suggest that "Pain, is about caring too much / For a carefree and deviant world".

The humanist interest visibly stops at some point and a new wave or movement of thought is taken up beginning with the poem "The Sex Allegory", which happens to be the title poem. From this poem onward, the poet seems to have been possessed by a sexist and feminist muse, and the poems that follow appreciate issues of womanhood, marriage and sexually in daring and challenging ways. Looking at the woman and appraising her has often been considered as a male function aimed at positioning the woman in an objectified weaker position because the man does the gazing. But in this collection, the poet changes or even reverses the position of focalization and does the gazing and appreciation of the feminine sublime, thereby allowing woman to appreciate womanly issues in a fashion that shows close affinity to the philosophies of renowned poets like Carol Anne Duffy.

The poems show a firm grasp of poetic connoisseurship, remarkable interests and broad range of style. They show fresh passion and a skilful mixture of charm and truthfulness in a lucid way. This is a must read collection especially for those interested in radical female ideologies or positions.

**Oscar C. Labang**
*Poet and Critic*

# Contents

# LOOK AT THE SLUMPS OF THE EARTH!

Look at the slumps of the earth!
Slimy and flowing ominously
Sluggishly over the earth
Leaving a permanent stench in the air

Oh you slumps of life,
You rub off your filth
On clean and unsuspecting mortals
You infest man with greed and unscrupulous intent.
Some are bound to suffer,

The unfortunates of the earth
Are branded slimy
While the real filth is hidden
Under the cloaks of affluence

How innocents suffer
Just because they wear
Poverty-tagged garments
Slumps of the earth
Can we ever wash you clean?

# WHY ARE WE SO BLESSED?

Why are we so blessed?
We run, skip and dance
We see and appreciate
The beauty of nature

Did we ever pause to ask
Why are we so blessed?
Did the cripple commit a crime to be thus punished?
Or did the deaf, blind and dumb perpetrate an act
To be thus maimed?

Do you look at yourself
And wonder what you did
To be so abundantly blessed?
Give thanks no matter the situation
Never count toes in the presence
Of those with only NINE.

## WANTING

Wanting, what a word
I want, I want and want again
Those forbidden things
Things I crave so bad for.
Wanting, how it plagues me
What is within reach
I don't want because
They are easy to get.
What comes in sincerity
I don't care about
I scoff at them, all I want
Are those tantalizing things
That are so out of reach,
Those are the things I try so hard to get
I weep because
I can't lay my hands on them.
These things at my feed, I discard
Because they are available
So why do I crave researchable things,
Yearn for unattainable heights?
It comes back to me now
As it did to Eve in Eden
FORBIDDEN things are sweetest
And things gotten the hard way
Are better appreciated and cherished
Oh wanting, how I want;
My cravings become the albatross around my neck.

## WEIGHT OF THE WORLD

When the world is against you
And you feel like you
Can't help it anymore
Be there for yourself
Don't let it engulf you in its darkness

If nobody needs you
Don't be perplexed.
You have many needs
Of which you need
Yourself to accomplish

If nobody loves you
Love yourself,
Believe in you
And you will be fulfilled
Be the most contented
No matter the odds,
Never lose faith in You.

## HEAD OF HEADS

If wishes were horses
I'll wish to become a president
An African president, to be precise
They are not answerable to anyone
They travel at will, they live abroad
Spend money like water.

If wishes were horses
I'll wish to become an African president
Because my relatives will be
Ministers without merit,
They will be awarded PhDs in the guise of regional
balance
I will not spare a thought for the masses
What if they remain poor and miserable?
It will keep them in their place.

If wishes were horses
I'll wish to become a president, an AFRICAN
president
Because I will be the Law
I'll be the head of everything that needs heading
Head of:
Armed forces,
Party,
State;

Head of heads

If wishes were horses
I will be an African president
Because the state is myself
And I am its driving force
I will bring forth Grand Ambitions
In fact it's just a matter of time.

## WHEN I LOOK AT OTHERS

When I look at others
Looking seemingly happy
Smiling even when there's
Nothing worth smiling
About, I ask why the hypocrisy?

Why can't I be like them
Who will smile when they
Really mean to cry?
Why can't I pretend
That all's bliss?
While
 I'm walking on hot coals
And not a drop of water
To soothe my distress?

## WHAT A WORLD

Some are going up
Others are coming down
Somewhere it is stagnant
As if paused by the great unknowable

Some watch this cacophony with confusion
Without understanding what is happening
They are so lost in this world of commotion
And they cry; what a world! What a world!

Some are catalyst of chaos
They spark uprisings everywhere
While the helpless and vunerable
Watch this cataclysm, awed
Not knowing where to turn
As every step is obstructed
By chaos

What a world! What a world!
I ponder in my amazement.
Is there no place for the weak and helpless?
No reward for goodness unless you are ruthless?

## MAN VS WOMAN

What makes a man is
The alacrity in the man
And what makes a woman is
The aura in the woman
Be it aura or alacrity,
It amounts to integrity
Integrity,
Seen in the manner of compunction
Rated as good or evil
People will either detest or love you
If you are well liked, then lucky you
It will be evident in the things they say
If you are detested, you are a social outcast
Your money could buy respectability depending
On how much you are worth,
but if you are bold enough
Give a damn, lucky you,
If you don't
You need to start over again

From aura or alacrity.

## POVERTY

I know no other word but destitute.
There is nothing to keep body and soul
By grace and mercy I survive
God's time is the best, let them say.

Lucky is he who wants.
He only lacks the means to support
He can live on hope
Though he will still die starving

Blessed is he who is relatively deprived.
He has feet but mourns the lack of shoes
He needs more for preservation
Not to feel poor, compared with others

## LAWS

Laws are made by man
To suit his purpose and needs
Make them, break them
Man live by man

A sailor on going to sea,
Had God's commandments under his belt
Because he was a great upholder of The Law
Yet, he deleted the Seventh. To steal
And plunder was his mission.

A lawyer went to court
Was asked to repeat the Lord's Laws
He omitted the Eighth. To bare false witness
Was the raison d'être of the session.

A leader changed the constitution
He consulted no one but the Good Lord
No one questioned the Supreme because
L'etat c'est lui même!
The law must favour its maker.

## YOUR EXCELLENCY

Blood! Blood on your hands
Civil strife is the tiger on whose tail
You ride to POWER.
Look at your hands, Excellency,
Blood of the innocents,
Tears of the oppressed,

Where is the much celebrated speech power?
Hunger, frustration and disillusionment glares
On the faces of the masses. They are dying,
Your Excellency, yet remain courageous
They carry on, in the face of your tyranny.

The masses are perishing, Excellency!
Watch out for you might become a ruler
Without a people. You swap on the opposition
Like a vulture, you'll make the nation a ghost town
For we all are your opposition
Your Excellency, power is not to monopolize
Remember Amin, Mubutu, Ali and Mubarak and
Learn the lesson, power is addictive and destroys.

## PAIN

It's all about being hurt
It's about being alone
It's about being on the edge
Of the world with nobody
To ask why you remain in the cold.

Pain, is about caring too much
For a carefree and deviant world
It's about loving a heartless human zombie
It's about losing your sense of direction
It's about being lost in a madding crowd
It's a way of life, it's the opposite ---.

## THE SEX ALLEGORY

What a flux,
Men and women wish
To out run each other in a race.
Men want something for free:
Fresh faces and variety makes life more fun
They stack preys with wads of cash - sweet nothings
But they are all vultures hovering over carcass.

Ladies know men have learned
The shooting trade so well,
They, the little birds,
Have learned the flying game too,
And practiced to filch grains in mid-flight.
They experiment their wiles and manoeuvres
On the placid fools, attempting to squeeze
Money out of tight fists.
Dangling their bodies for bait,
Men too, fabricate means to get it free.
Who wins is irrelevant. It's an ancient game:
Same routine, same strategy, new faces.

Sometimes, the old pot-belly sugar papas
More enthusiastic than the young dudes,
Totally discredit the aged adage - grey is wisdom,
But promote the more appealing other –
Libido is like wine, it matures with age.

14

## SHATTERED ILLUSIONS

Nothing is what it seems.
It's hard to follow the trend of life;
A vessel in which nothing is
Permanent but change…
One sees a surface glitter,
It's gold for sure,
Investigation,
It's nothing but glittery filth.
Shattered illusions

Two people come together
In love, they say.
They seem inseparable
Yet, they look irreconcilable
One is North, the other is South.
Shattered illusions!

Why can't things ever be real?
Why must they seem to be what
They will never be?
Is it fate that plays on man
Or does man trick himself with mirages
Reality is harsh but
Shouldn't we confront it sometimes?

## LONELINESS

Nobody knows what it really means
To be lonely but a woman, a deserted one
Loneliness is an illness
That takes one unawares and in unlikely places
It can pounce on you in a crowd.

Nobody feels the pinch of loneliness
Like a woman: especially a woman in love
You become lonely when the man you love
Is not interested in you,
Loneliness is your bedfellow
When that man you yearn for won't glance
Your way no matter what you do to catch his gaze
You taste loneliness
When he behaves as though you were invisible.

Nobody can really tell you what
Loneliness is, but a childless widow,
She smells loneliness when that man
Who used to be the king in her world is gone
She walks hand in glove with loneliness
When she puts on a new dress and no one compliments

## NINE QUESTIONS

Why are fingers not equal?
Can it be that the maker feared rivalry?
Why are some black and others white?
Does it mean the creator is a lover
Of variety and not discrimination?

How can mathematicians say
One plus one plus one equals three
Yet the bible refutes because
One plus one plus one equals one
How can religions say man is
Made in God's image, yet Darwin
Claims man is the predecessor of an ape.

Why are some poor, others rich?
Yet they work as hard, if not harder
Could it be that some are children of
A lesser god?
Is there justice in the world?
Why are the minorities, the deprived
Discriminated upon?
The truth certainly lies
In numbers, gender, and status

Nothing is what it seems;
Ideologies crop up like the undergrowth

Philosophers come and go,
Believes die with their acolytes,
The poor remain poor if not poorer,
Still no one gives a damn about prophets.

## LIFE

Gift of gold shimmering like the sun,
It makes its way from dawn to down
Bright as the rainbow on a cloudy horizon,
Gift of life, given freely to man
Who knows not its worth

Life! Beautiful gift of Mother Nature
Given to us folks without conditions
What becomes of it, depends on the
Individual in question, or destiny

Life, the essence of mankind
Friend to those who know diplomacy
And enemy to he who tries
To dabble and toss about

## TO LOVE AND LOST

It's better not to have loved than to lose it
It's the pain of spending a day in paradise to wake in
hell
It's a nightmare you might never wake from.
If you aren't capable of cherishing and keeping love
It's better not to dapple with it,
Its hurt like you can never imagine.

## NOW I KNOW

Now I know
I've been chasing shadows all my life
I heard that something existed like this,
I had doubts; I've searched the nooks and crannies
Of this world without finding it

Now I know that all
My life I've been searching for you
Yet, you were just round the corner
But my vision was tainted

Now that I have finally found you
I won't let you go for all the gold
Of Ghana or the diamonds in Congo
Because my world will be bleak without you

I know happiness is intermittent
But I will take my chances,
I will keep you for as long as it takes
All the difficult moments will only spice our bliss.

## THE FOOL

The fool says
I am important, rich
And influential, I'm on top of the world.
 I'm the envy of friends
The dread of enemies,
To be rich is beautiful. You live by your own ethics.
Only the poor must be decorous and humble
The least of their indiscretions are exposed
My rich friends and I float in a bubble of serenity
It is another dimension, you can only appreciate
If you have the aura which only money can instate
Your word is law and everyone works like ants
To please you. What bliss to be rich and connected!
Money is power and power is sweeter than nectar.
Whoever says money can't buy everything
Doesn't know where to shop.

## POINT OF ATTRACTION

Na me I fine so
Papa G thank you
I be good trader, I use
What I have to get what I need
With my few talents, I take times
Papa, na you sef talkam,
So when I waka comot
I di make statement
Dress to kill, na ma policy.
My spaghetti blouse leaves nothing to fancy
I use the pop up bra, and shiny makeup
To multiply my chances
My first point of attraction.

Never leave a stone unturned or
An opportunity unexplored, that na
Ma second motto.
Since I got the front covered
Time to concentrate on the backside,
That na the real blessing wey African woman get
Our own round, then e hilly like
the corners of Eve's apple
Papa G thank you say our own no flat
like fufu whe dem slappam for wall.
When I take the corner with my
tight taille base jeans, traffic di stop,

All eyes di turn to my point of attraction
As I gyrate sensuously down the street.

Make we take the optional, insurance policy
Na the best, the third point is mostly muted
Like a side show, the first and second,
being too Strong  have stolen the limelight, but
Sometimes, you meet the rare type that is myopic
And see only my gape toothed smile, Chaucer
Says women like us are devious, luring the unwary
To their doom with that flash of glory,
This third point of attraction is important
In times of diplomacy, like when police try to ask
For I.D card whe you no get, just project the killer smile
It works like magic, bottom belly power na yi di win the
                                                                                 day.

Me too I be born again, when it's time for mass
I am the first to attend; I take the front seat, the vantage
Position for eye contact with him at the pulpit.
With my long tight skirt I can still project the rear end,
that fatal point of attraction.

I take the prize for being the best dancer,
If the man of God is single, all
The attention is for him,
If he isn't the other prosperous brothers will do
You can call me a church prostitute if you care,

Lighthouse Chapel, Winner's Wagon,
Jehovah wickedness… I have seen them all,
I don't entertain criticism because I know what
I want; time is not meant to waste,
If there isn't anything for me,
I clean the dust off my feet and
Move on to the next opportunity.

## BEAUTY IN A BOTTLE

Some are born beautiful
Others acquire beauty
Others have beauty imposed upon them
But these parameters are now out of context
Because we've got beauty in a bottle -
Liquid powder to build a strong foundation
Semi-liquid powder to make it last,
Shimmering blush to enhance the youthful hue.
Eye shadow is now colourful. Do the eye to fit
the mood - green hue, pink hue, smoky eye
*Goddess effect*, take your pick.

Ladies rejoice with me,
There are no longer ugly sisters
Thanks to beauty in a bottle
Portable and compact, mirror equipped
When there is need,
Do damage control and remain fresh
Thanks to beauty in the bottle.

## NIP/TUCK

Beauty is power which I must possess
At all cost, God I know you did a good job
And put doctors to make it perfection
Plastic surgeons, as logical as the tailor
Who will nip and tuck at the loose ends
The human prêt a porter dress.

I have a pretty enough face, but
Dr Rey will make it plastic perfect,
My nose is too stubby and
My lips are too thin, a little tightening here,
A few Botox shots will yield something Helen-like
There is no such thing like too much beauty.
This original design is open for modification
We need a few ornaments to pop out the dress.

Beyonce is blessed with a good sized ass
That is discrimination, but God I will regulate
That for you, no more jealousy ladies, Dr Dan
Is here, he gives generous behinds though to the
Bewilderment of drum stick legs,
Everyone is bootylicious,
We live happily ever after
And it sure fits so nicely in the dress.

My breast are so tried up, like cassava planted

In unyielding soil. I am tired of pop up bras,
I want more and it's possible Dr Pat is here.
He gives balls of silicon that can turn
Pamela Anderson green with envy,
Hers were picked from over the counter too
But the surgeon's skill makes them special

We are empowered but we fear to age
Cougar Town is skyrocketing
Because the Ancients have refused to age
Wife of Frankenstein carries the proof
Of plastic beauty gone awry, yet we won't accept
That natural beauty is best, we prefer the plastic dress.

## PUPPET MASTER

You pull the strings and
We dance to the tune
You make us shameless in
Our greed to grab and rob.
We'll say and do anything
If the price is right.
Ministers are decreed to play
The fool, they are now jest masters
Who will thank the Head of State
 Even for the air they breathe
Puppet master, you make a mockery of PhDs,
They turn to clowns and give vaudeville acts
To affirm your hold on the puppet collar around their
necks.

## CHIC MADAM

Chic Madam, you look so
Cool, totally decked up, you are
The fashion icon, only that the trends
You set are a little too expensive to follow,
That horse hair or (does it belong to a poor Indian?)
Looks a trifle too heavy to carry. How many packets
Did you off-load? I bet you have a stiff neck every day
But that is fashion, it totally hurts to be the queen of glam.

Those stilettos could break an ankle
How many centimetres? Mami you are
Courageous, aren't they supposed to make us
Look elegant and chic? But the way you stumble,
The mask of pain that reflects in your expression,
Does not tell such a tale. What if they were a little nearer
To the ground, would the 'sti' disappear from the
'tos'?
I know beauty hurts, but we shouldn't maim the feet in
This race for glam.

The lightening lotion that you use
Must be the best, for first you had a hue
Of bronze that mark that beautiful race of Cleopatra
Then sooner you became a little too peachy but still
Recognizable, but now you are totally red, switching

Camps and hard to classify. All in all you look
spectacular
Groomed like a Barbie, dumb as a nail, I see a semblance-
A rough plan in the maze of conflicting styles
competing
Shine out the other, colour riot is the end result. Watch!
Give not the fashion police a warrant to arrest you in this
race for glam.

## WHAT'S A BOOK?

Blank pages waiting to be filled by a scribbler
scribble on, like all the others throughout time.
you are neither on the left nor right
so bare, no scruples, defame and praise - when you please
the creed of the unscrupulous writer
to speak extensively on the issue of the day - little facts.
You need not investigate the crust of the matter.
Good writing is a waste of time; half-truths are more
interesting than the facts.
Take up the burning issue of the day
Learn a few facts about the matter
Repeat them constantly and with authority
That my friend will make you a writer
and what you scribble a book,
maybe

## WEDDING MARCH

### *Bride:*

Finally this blissful day has arrived
angels shall descend from heaven, I'm certain,
the priest is ready, the congregation is waiting,
I am the envy of all my friends
(every bride thinks her friends envy her)
the stage is set, everything perfect; all I need is to say
"I do"
the day of my triumphant entry into Matt's house
(after a lot of scheming and intrigue)
all those guys who hurt me in the past, shame on you!
all those girls who bitched at me and said this will
never happen,
who is laughing now?
I am in tenth heaven but I'm a little worried for my
husband to be,
he has this constipated look on his face
"darling are you alright?"

### *Groom:*

"Yes my love, I am alright," replied the unhappy groom
Ok, yes I'm happy. It's my wedding day isn't it?
 I'm happily worried about the outcome.
the loan is going to take years to pay off,
about this marriage, am I doing the right thing?
is Jessica the one for me?

but she kind of looks real good in that white garb
though I think the white dress is a cliché
isn't it supposed to indicate virginity?
that is a laugh, this lady has seen a lot of action
and now she is wearing a million dollar smile.
she must be congratulating herself for
shackling and dragging me to the altar.
And now I have to say "I do"
and pledge myself for ever after,
"I do" to sickness, "I do" to meanness,
to fatness and all the other nesses.
"I do" what the hell, there is no turning back now.

## SUITORS

"I am a poet and you're a poetess,
I love thee well, will you be my muse." Says the suitor
I am a poet just like you and not
A poetess, I won't be your muse.
If anything I will be your mentor,
You put me in a place I strife to surpass
You go with the claim that we are weaker
Unequal to man yet you claim to be in love, if we can't
Be equals I won't succumb to accept a cause
That will only shackle me like a curse
I know your intentions, I will not be enslaved.

Here comes another… he looks so hyped
He's in the best suit and is my suitor
He comes with a ring but holds a noose
Behind his back, he has a tale which we must tell
Women shouldn't be too educated
(they make the man feel inferior)
What they should do is know the minimal …
What pleases a man. Here
The man is king, a good wife assuages his ego -.
You should be lucky that I selected you from all the lot
Women are in droves so you shouldn't be proud,
you should be glad… you got the hour of day.
Educated women never marry
Because they're too full of the white man's nonsense,
I am giving you the chance, to have a man. A private king,
To do his bidding and be a complete woman.

I beg to pass, that's my answer,
I won't have you, for all the diamonds
In the Congo, you think you're hype that isn't true,
You're narcissistic
I won't have you, if this was the desert
And you the last drop of water.
Where I come from women are Queens
And are so treated, every woman has a right to - - -
Humility is probity we learn in class, you aren't much of
man
So you need a slave to boost your ego,
You try to colonise me in the name of marriage…

The next of note was such a player,
he's scored so many goals in his time
Now he's in love with me.
That's a joke; a bad boy is a bad boy.
They never change.
This one has seen beneath all women
In his sight and some other doubtful characters
He plays the marriage card
because he thinks it will pull me in the game
He says he's changed but his eyes proof the lie, -
One lady to the other, undressing us as we walk the street.
Talk of harassment
He should be arrested, he is a time bomb.
He comes back to the point,
"would you have my heart, I want to be yours forever."
Sorry I'm cool, I don't want your heart.
I doubt you have one worth a dime!
What of all the sisters you've been through,

those you've broken in your race
I might have you on one condition to be really sure.
Write a national apology to all my sisters,
those you've hurt and those you've derailed. Be ready -
Pay indemnity, most will need hearts transplant.
When you're done and you're still
In love, we will harvest your eyes for your own good.
It is better to enter the kingdom
Of heaven maimed than to go to hell a handsome dude.


The next on the pedestal is the school teacher,
you have mastered the art of skirt chasing. Like a dementor,
He feeds on fear and pounce when the target is weak, STM
He doles out like the Good Samaritan.
He's my suitor too, the act of intimidation
Doesn't work for me, I was a lot more intrigued by his head
                              of wit.
Overruled by the little fool he nurses between his legs.
Dark corners… Sleazy motels…
He knows them all, he will have you or you're out.
Blame not the player … But the game…
He's just a man, that specie is weak and liable to
                              temptation.
Though one so sage, the pull is strong,
He will play the fool not out of choice
Since Adam, the fairer sex has been the man's Achilles'
                              heel.


The next in line is the sugar daddy,
his belly competes only with the size of his wallet.
he wants it all, another trophy to hang on his wall,

he's rich he can afford it.
Give him a chance and he would take you places,
he will spoil you but don't get used to it,
Be sure that he will drop you
without a backward glance when he smells another trophy.
This money bag is a hopeless romantic;
he yearns for youthful freshness to cover his aging
He'll harvest the stars and give you in a bouquet
and other such vanities just to lure you
He wants my heart, he'll settle for nothing less,
be my deviation he is quick to ask
You'll have the best whenever you see me,
never call me no matter the problem
I'll get to you when the need be,
I know it's a shame to court the cot
But I'm a man and needs to play.
The temptation is great but still I'll pass.
You've lived your life and now is my turn
In the business of hearts cash is not the exchange,
you need a heart to bargain for one
And live the stars in the sky as they are,
that is nature for everyone to enjoy.

# THESE FEMINIST CLOWNS

We are feminist clowns, those of us who
Chatter like waver birds, making grand schemes
Of how to kill the man and rule the world.
No concrete solutions!!!
We are all talk.
We don't see the root of the problem
We all blame MAN.
Patriarchy was born by men. Yet,
Woman is the guidance and nurturer through ages
Who holds a woman down to mutilate
But another woman!
Who connives with men to bring a strong woman down
If not another woman?
Who marries into another woman's home, and wreck
Havoc on a fellow sister
Is it not another woman?
Real feminists ask for equal rights; not many more license
Real feminists seek to educate the woman; give them hope
They don't move the motion to mutilate manhood
We still need to procreate even from sperm donor banks.
They acquaint with the current issues of the nations
They build the nation and not rock it foundations.
Real feminists don't attempt schemes un applicable
To their cultural backgrounds.
Real feminists nurture families; spend time with kids
Real feminists know their strengths,
They don't need to wear the Pants to show they're strong.

## DONS PLAYING POLITICS

Leave politics to the politicians
You are a don, it's not your place
To make a fool of the great institutions of learning.
Leave politics to the politicians, a don's
Place is on the Left and not in the Right. It's your
Pride of place to criticize grand ambition, regional
Balance, the employment of the starving twenty-five.
Leave politics to the politicians, you can't be at peace
With the few francs that exchange hands, like thirty pieces
this time not to sell another, but to kill your conscience.
We have no roads, talk about that, we have no system,
Open their eyes, to the chaos, we have no peace,
Tell them that the absence of war does not signify harmony.
Leave politics to the politician, you are the social
                                        conscience,
We are still marginalised, make them aware.
We have been played the fool, it's partly our faults.
Leave politics to the politicians, force them to see the light,
The ignorant prefers the cave, but we're at the margin of the
global village. The glare of the spotlight reaches us yet.
Let's open our eyes to the mess
The plight of youth, the rape of innocence, the stench of
                                        corruption.

## CONFESSIONS OF A COUGAR VICTIM

My name is Sam, it rhymes with Sand
I am a victim and I must report this injustice
Is hard to bare. I am a Mama's boy everyone
Knows. I have been assaulted my innocence taken
Down with the Cougar, I was the guiles victim in the
                                        quick sand.


Like young piglets suckling gleefully she pounces
On me, as thirsty labourers takes to oranges she makes
Me a husk, I was an innocent, thinking Mama
Was just caring for all the children of the world as
                                        most mothers do
But she was strategizing, she had me eating
Out of her hand in no time then of a sudden she
pounced.


She turned into a tigress, after coming forth as a
nurturer
Sympathiser with the plight of the youth as hopeless
She only saw her margin shifting, debunking her
Position and renaming her a has been,
She took the radar and lured me into her trap
With songs of fecundity, and naive me,
Thinking of my dear mother believed this was
nurturing.

41

Shameless Cougar! Allow the youth to grow,
Their problems are numerous,
they don't have Jobs,
don't add to the disillusionment.
You use your Big cars like honey to catch flies,
You project fake smiles to lure the innocence,
Mothers should bless and not be a
Curse that traumatise the young and inhibit their
growth.

## HAIL THE PROPHETS

Hail holy Joshua, hail the prophet
The author of miracles, the modern saint
Hail the man of God, Emmanuel! He's with us
Hope of the hopeless, staff of the cripple, the
Man of God, hail the teacher the envy of his kind!
Healer of the sick, the emissary of goodwill, comforter
Of widows,   we have spinsters no more, hail the great one
It's his due, salvation is personal but still there's always a
prize


While we're hailing let's hail Chris, he is a great Bishop
And a modern day dude. His coat is of the best quality.
Bishop's
Grammar is flawless, the congregation should upgrade,
his sermons
Are spectacular he dazzles us all. He's such a gift, a gifted
man
Of God! Sterile wombs are fertilised, blind men see,
Chris is a performer
We're spell bound by his art, we look at his pointed shoes
and envisage
The days of old when Christ walked. Holy Ghost fire!
It's the time of the Spirit,
Father and Son are relegated, old orders change.
Gone are the days of bread and water.


They've spread like wildfires as foretold,

The Holy Book insists
Christ is not a monopoly of the Jews -
The word must spread to the Gentiles
The harvest is plentiful labourers are few, so we look to
                              the Spirit to choose
His helpers, though most seem uncouth and misquote the
                              scriptures. But they
Provide enthusiasm where there is want of sense, Chris is
                              an icon, Joshua a sage.
Give us miracles that is all we ask for,
we'll like to ride though we never work for a spook
Give us miracles we dearly want such,
though we embezzle and cripple the nation
Let's have miracles this is the time, …
Pentecostal wins the day…
We all need miracles even when they're fake.

## GREEN MEMORIES

As a child I wandered lonely
As the cloud in Wordsworth's melody
The fields were green and the air as fresh
Live was beautiful then it's certain, the only
Inhabitants that shared my world was nature: the hum
Of the bee, singing their contentment as they kissed
The wild flowers that added colour to that dappled
Beauty.

Green is a backdrop for nature's canvas
Not even Da Vinci or Reynolds with all
Their genius could picture it as perfect as it
Once was. Yellow flowers smile at the sun in the
morn,
Tiny violets play their part, the Queen of
the Night perfumes the air. As a child I will
Pause and breathe, marvelling at his work so
Great, as the chime of the bell from the Emmanuel
Sisters clank in harmony as if to affirm the unspoken
Thought.

As a child I would marvel at the tall green
Elephant grass that kept it's green even in
The harmattan, in whose folds multicoloured beetles
Would make their home,
I walk the route again

45

But all is gone, no more beautiful fields
To walk and dream, sterile houses and deserts
Of yards have taken the space. Mother nature
Is at bay, she weeps aloud but we drown her wails
With the heavy drones of expensive vehicles
That corrupts the air, with the stench of blood-stained
Fuel.

## MONT FEBE: THE FOUNT OF NATURE

Mont Febe, fount of nature, pretty
As a picture. I stand on your pinnacle
And enjoy the bliss that only you can give
You present a bird's view, of what destruction
Modernism has wrecked my town.  The monstrosity of urban
Life is humming a distant jingle on this abyss of peace
City dwellers with country souls, worn your parts
to derive the regeneration which only you can bring

Surprise to see your forest still standing, like the last of the
                                                        Knights
In great Camelot, when ancestral groves have all been
                                                    desecrated
By greedy protectors in search of cash. Walls get thorn
                                                down for the
Desire of fresh air, our natural beauty suffers for France to
                                                    have wood
Our leaders will make an exchange of anything to boost
                                                    their egos,
Mount Febe, the fount of nature, I fear the saw will soon
                                                fall, when greedy
Maniacs who will barter anything for a bit of green in their
                                                        pockets,
Discover your immense treasure.
Mont Febe! Fount of Nature,
When the heat of urbanisation stifles my thoughts
And turn me into a mass of nerves,
I think of your three green slopes and drink inspiration.

## FIRST LINE INDEX